YOU Are Smart & YOU Are Strong

Laura Harris

Illustrated by Corinne Harris

Copyright © 2015 Laura Harris

ISBN-13: 978-0692545294 (Laura Harris)
ISBN-10: 0692545298

DEDICATION

This book is lovingly dedicated to all the children of the world.

Sometimes, older kids or adults do bad things to children that hurts them.

Sometimes, older kids or adults treat children like they are their girlfriend or boyfriend.

Sometimes, older kids or adults treat children like they are their husband or wife.

They might kiss you in a romantic way.

They might touch any part of your body in a romantic way or touch your private body parts (like your penis, vagina, butt, chest, breast, lips, or mouth).

They might show you or ask you to touch or kiss parts of their own body that are usually covered up by underwear or a bathing suit.

They might ask to see, touch, or kiss parts of your body that are usually covered up by underwear or a bathing suit.

They might have you be naked or in your underwear and take pictures or movies of you.

They might show you pictures or movies of adults or kids doing any of these things.

There are other things that may happen to you that are bad and hurt you, so if you ever have a question, be sure to ask an adult.

These things are bad, and these things hurt children. It is called Sexual Abuse and NOBODY should be doing any of these things with you.

These things may not have always been happening or may not be going on all the time, but even ONE time is bad because it hurts you.

Even if any of these things are happening with someone in your family, it is bad.

Even if any of these things are happening with someone who is a friend or relative of your family, it is bad.

Even if any of these things are happening at home, at school, at church, at sports, or ANYWHERE, it is bad.

Even if any of these things are happening with someone you like or love, it is bad.

It is bad because

Sexual Abuse

hurts children!

These things sometimes
might make you feel
warm inside or might
make you feel love.

Your feelings are not bad,
but what is happening to
you is hurting you.

You are good. Even if bad things are happening to you,

YOU ARE GOOD!

You are also SMART, so I want to tell you that the person doing these things to you is playing a very mean trick on you.

Are you confused?

I know I was confused
when Sexual Abuse was
happening to me.

Here is how to not be confused. Ask yourself, "Is this a secret?"

If it is a secret, then it is bad. If it is a secret, then it is hurting you.

If the person doing these Sexual Abuse things to you tells you that you will get into trouble if you tell or even if you FEEL like you might get into trouble if you tell, these are more tricks!

One out of every three girls have Sexual Abuse happen to them.

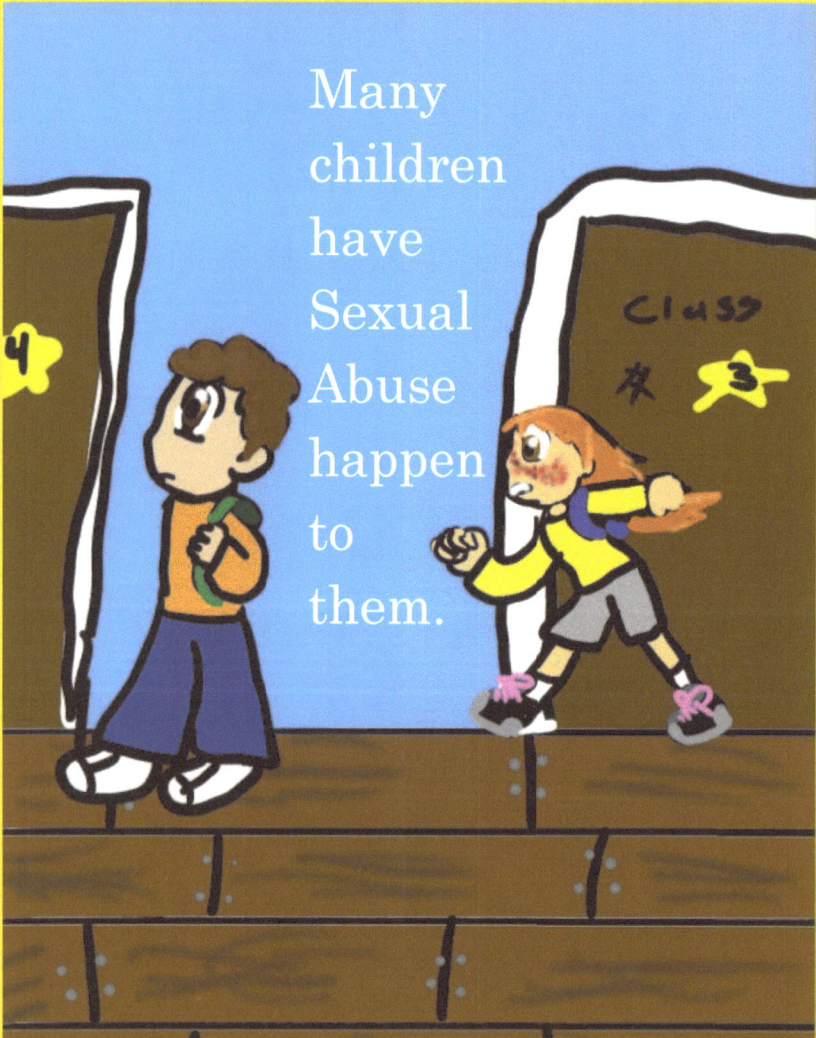

Many children have Sexual Abuse happen to them.

One out of every six boys have Sexual Abuse happen to them.

Sexual Abuse can happen to anyone! It can happen:

no matter where in the world you live;

no matter what type of house or neighborhood you live in;

no matter how much money your parents make;

no matter what color your skin is.

It can happen when you are alone with another person, or it can happen when there are others in the very same room.

YOU are smart & YOU are strong,
so I will tell you more.

Often, children do not know they are being hurt, because they do not know enough facts about Sexual Abuse.

When children do not know or understand that they are being hurt or when they are being tricked or feel afraid, they usually do not tell anybody to stop hurting them and they do not tell anybody they are being hurt.

Then, the older kid or adult continues the Sexual Abuse for a long time, hurting them more and more.

No one helps these children, because it is a secret. No one knows these children need help to stop the Sexual Abuse.

Secrets like Sexual Abuse cause big damage to a child's mind and soul.

So, as they grow up, the hurt from the secret can stay with them, unless they ask for and receive help.

Because of the Sexual Abuse that happened to them when they were children:

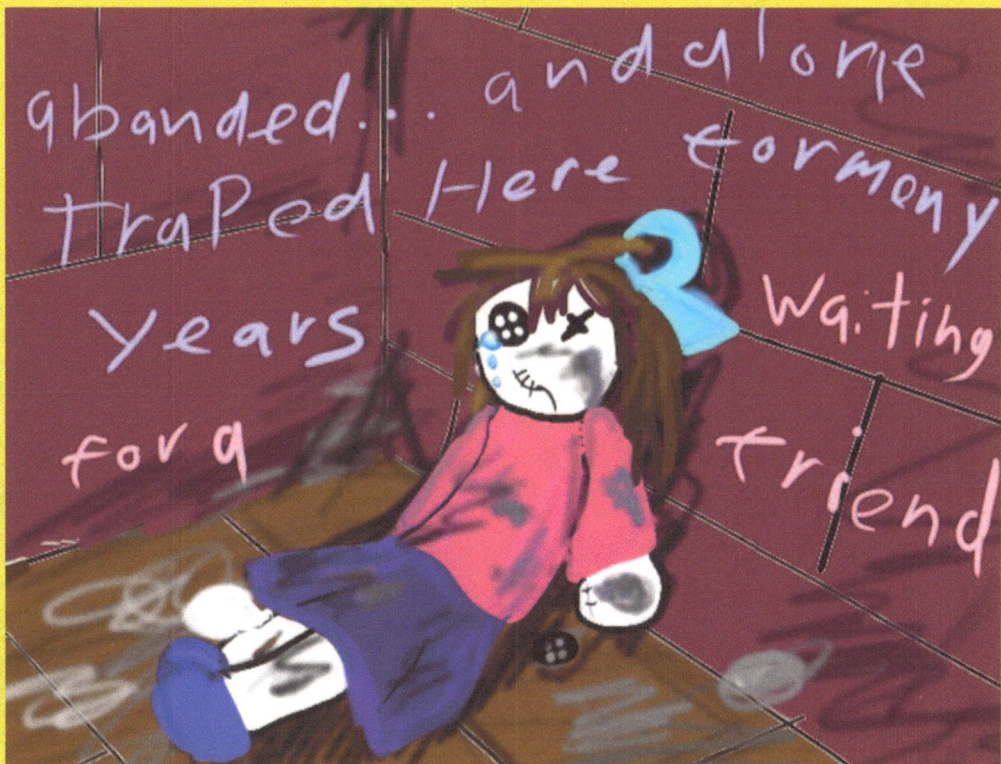

abanded... and alone
traped Here for many
years   waiting
for a   friend

Some become addicted to drugs.
Some are not able to have a family.
Some who do have a family cannot
take care of their children.
Some are not able to have a job.
Some are not able to be happy.
Some become homeless.
Some become very, very sick.
Some die.

These bad and terrible things should not happen to you now or as you grow up. Sexual Abuse is bad and terrible. All the things that might happen to you when you grow older because of the Sexual Abuse are bad and terrible.

ONLY good should happen to you!

YOU are STRONG. So,
you can use your voice.
Use your voice to say,

"STOP HURTING ME!"

You can also use your voice to tell someone that you are being hurt by Sexual Abuse.

Tell your teacher; tell your mom; tell your dad; tell your neighbor.

But, just be sure to tell an adult who is not hurting you. Tell an adult who is not doing the Sexual Abuse to you.

If you tell, and it keeps happening, then find another person to tell.

This is VERY important. You
can use your voice to say,

"I AM BEING HURT! PLEASE HELP ME!"

If your voice won't work,
you can write a note and
give it to an adult.

Telling someone is VERY important, because then you will stop being hurt, and you can get the help you need, like counseling or therapy.

It is also VERY important to use your voice this way, because other children may be being hurt now by the same person, or other children will be hurt in the future.

People who do Sexual Abuse to children do not just do it to ONE child.

You are not the only one.

YOU are smart
& YOU are strong!

Let all of us who are smart & strong use our voices to STOP the Sexual Abuse of children.

www.ingramcontent.com/pod-product-compliance
Lightning Source LLC
LaVergne TN
LVHW010026070426
835509LV00001B/28